T0161546

the *silent* Unwinding

an illustrated notebook for dreamers

JACKIE MORRIS

unbound

To all who have the courage to create,
for to create means to open the heart up
to the possibility of error and only
through making mistakes
can we learn.

This book is a companion to *The Unwinding*. It contains within it images that tell stories, but it reads like a silent film.

Each of the images is an invitation to dream, and where in *The Unwinding* the stories are pinned to the page by words, here they are free, fluid, evolving.

Shaped over time and in and out of years, at times when life became too constricting, too tight, each image was an unwinding for its maker, a way of easing the soul through shape, pigment and story.

The Silent Unwinding leaves space for its reader to shape their own dreams using these silent stories as a catalyst. The space can be filled with whatever you wish – image, word, collage – because the space is yours.

To facilitate this, ask yourself questions about the characters.

Who is the woman who wanders
the land with the bear and
her cart filled with books?

Why does the woman in the
yellow dress sleep so soundly
with the great white bear?

How does the midnight fish fly?

Where are they going, these people
who ride out from the woods?

When did they meet,
the girl and the wolves?

What became of the curious
boat that sailed the calm sea,
beneath the moon, so full
and round in the sky?

Because stories begin with questions, and questions seek answers.

Time is a curious creature, one that fascinates. And if the book were to be written again by the author, would the stories remain the same?

May your time in these pages be time spent well.

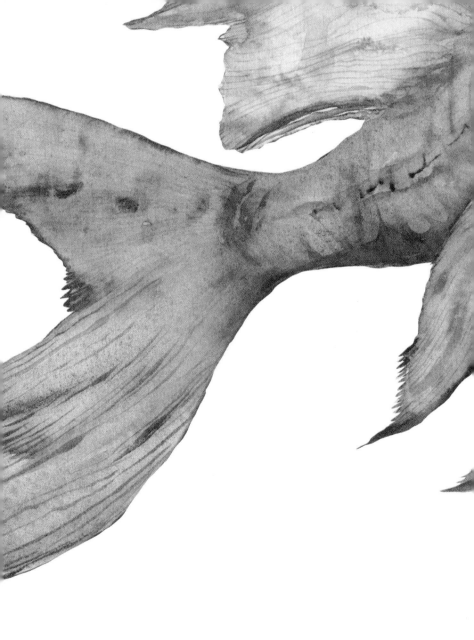

R est now,
in the peace of
the wild things.
May the swan be your pillow,
may the gold owl bring you visions.
May the red fox gift you cunning,
and the wolf bring you courage.

And may the white
horse lend her strength
to all your days.

ACKNOWLEDGEMENTS

With huge thanks to my agent, Jessica Woollard, for all the support and encouragement and for believing in me.

Also to Unbound, who see books as individual creatures, and especially to Lizzie Kaye, for understanding the curious pathways my mind wanders and for helping with the evolution of *The Unwinding*.

Thanks also to Alison O'Toole, designer, who listens, and then takes any ideas I may have had and then makes them as beautiful as they can be, with skill, and vision.

Thank you to everyone who pledged for this book, before they had even seen what it would be.

And also to the pack and the pride of those who share the days with me, Nicola Davies, who has taught me so much, and listens and knows when to offer advice and when to offer encouragement.

And to Robin… who always falls asleep when I read to him.

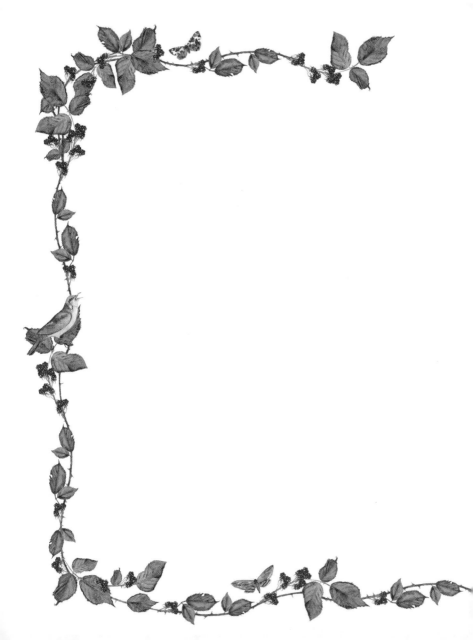

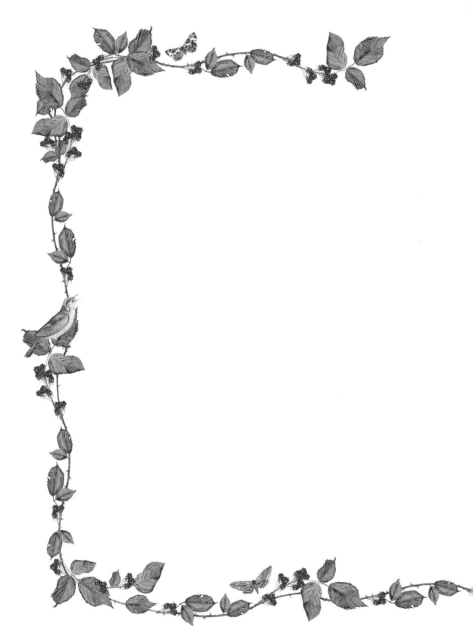

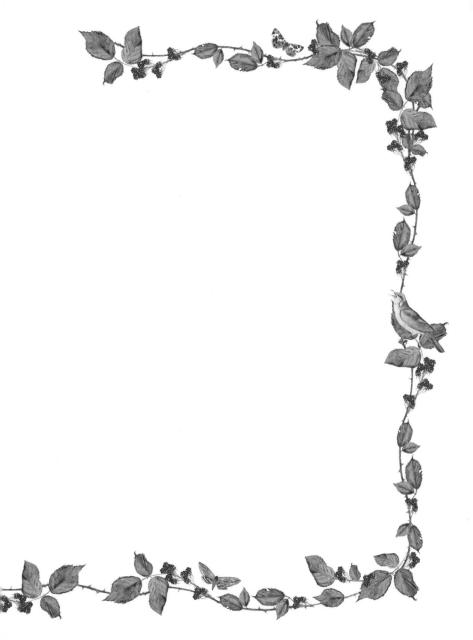

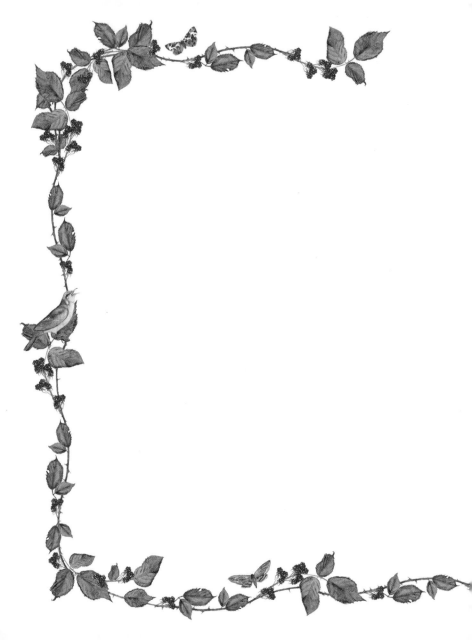

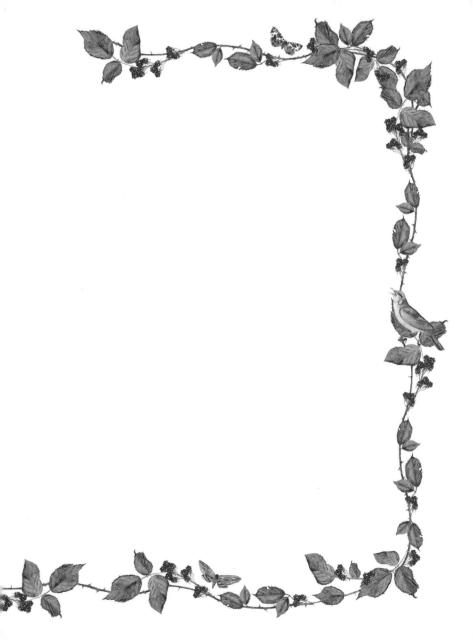

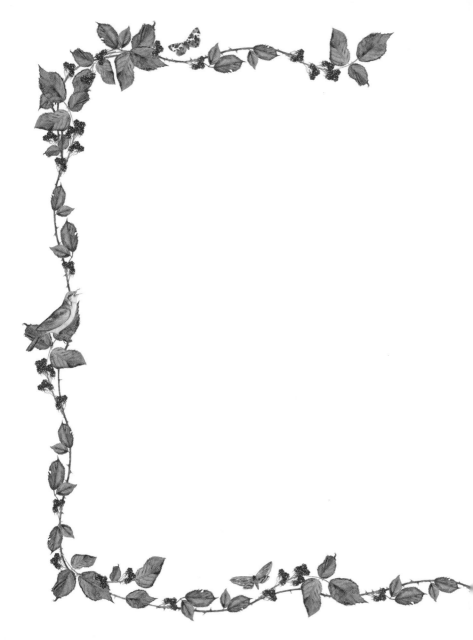

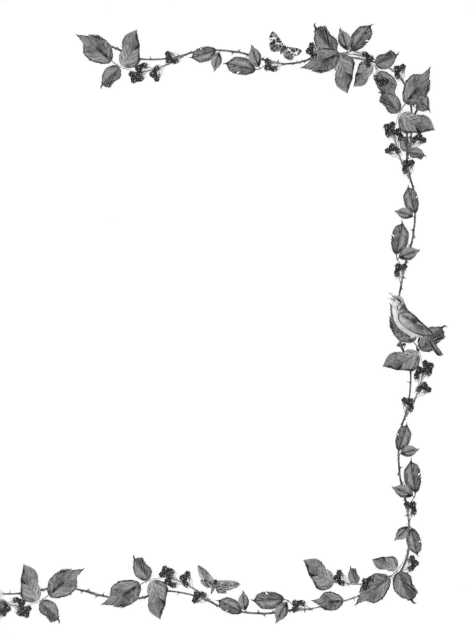

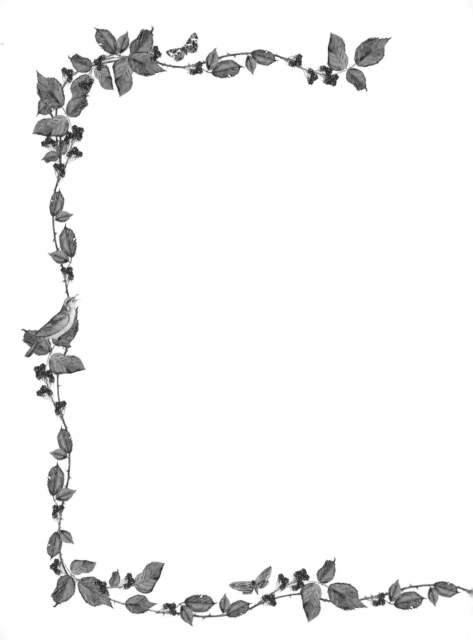

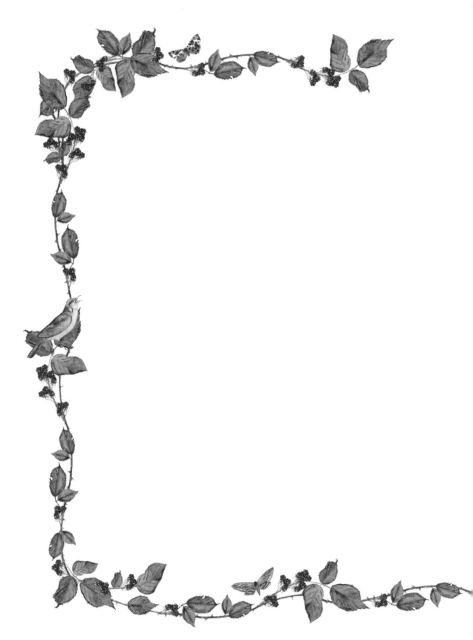

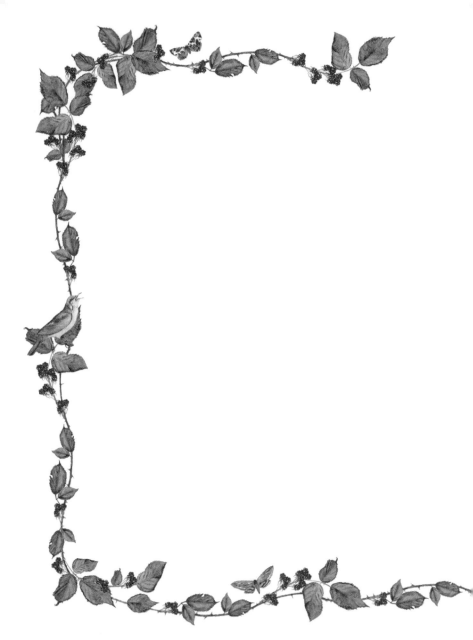

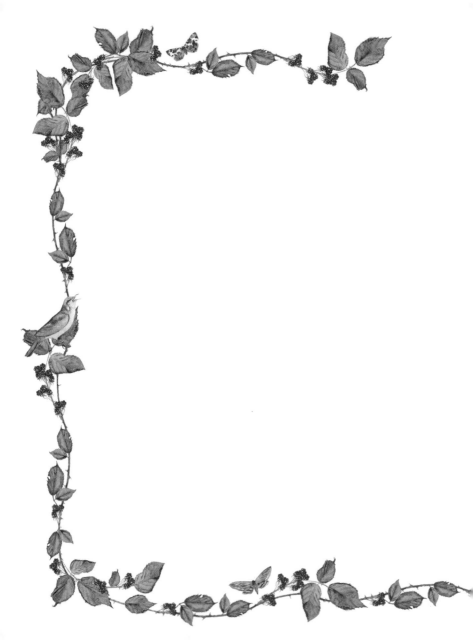

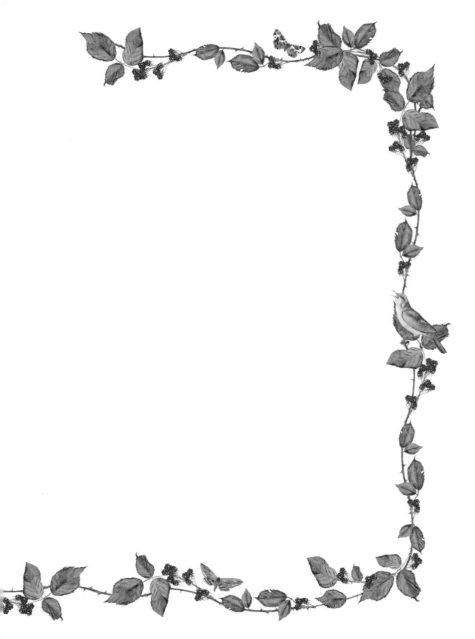

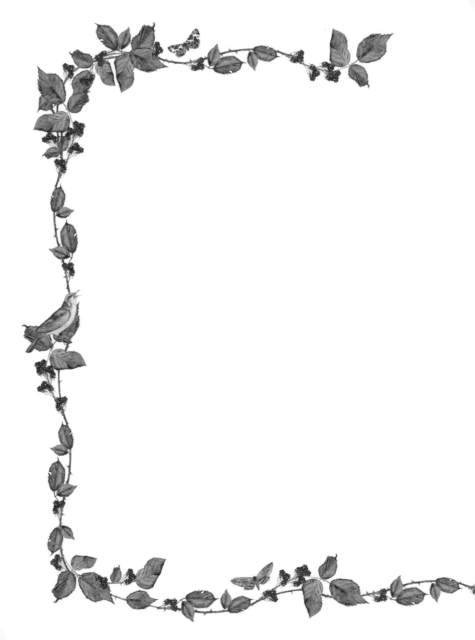

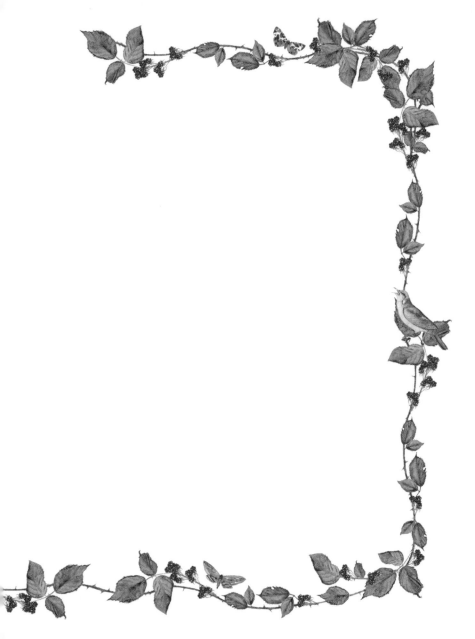

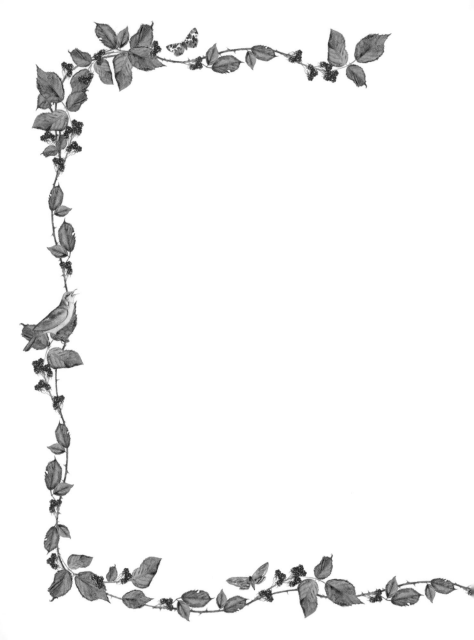

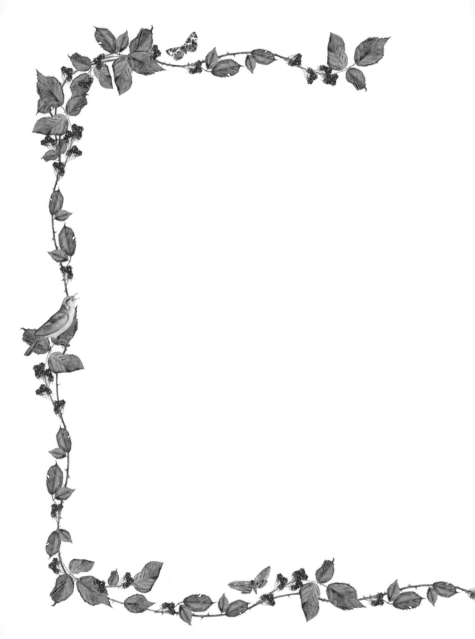

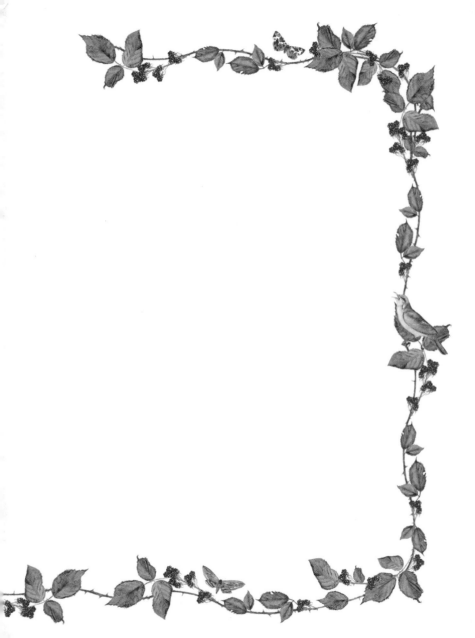

First published in 2020

Unbound

6th Floor Mutual House, 70 Conduit Street, London W1S 2GF

www.unbound.com

All rights reserved

Design by Alison O'Toole

Pages 8, 11–19, 23–33, 35–39, 43–49, 53–61, 65–71, 75–81,
85–91, 95–101, 105–111, 115–123, 125–131, 135–141, 145–151,
and 155–179 composed and remixed by Alison O'Toole.
These images © Alison O'Toole and Jackie Morris, 2020

A CIP record for this book is available from the British Library

ISBN 978-1-78352-935-3 (Trade edition)
ISBN 978-1-78352-935-3 (Special edition)
ISBN 978-1-78352-961-2 (Silent edition)

Printed in Slovenia by DZS Grafik

3 5 7 9 8 6 4